D1314565

12 TERRIFYING
MONSTERS

by Allan Morey

STORY
LIBRARY

www.12StoryLibrary.com

12-Story Library is an imprint of Peterson Publishing Company and Press Room Editions.

Produced for 12-Story Library by Red Line Editorial

Photographs ©: Fer Gregory/Shutterstock Images, cover, 1; Henry Fuseli, 4; Fritz Schwimbeck, 5; BERMANN, Moriz, 6; Andrew Rich/iStockphoto, 8, 29; shyflygirl/iStockphoto, 9; Big_Ryan/iStockphoto, 10; Alexlky/Shutterstock Images, 11; Serge_Vero/iStockphoto, 12; Vectorig/iStockphoto, 13; duncan1890/iStockphoto, 14; Mayor, Alfred Goldsborough, 1868-1922 New York Zoological Society, 15; TT/iStockphoto, 16; Matt84/iStockphoto, 17; fotofojanini/iStockphoto, 19, 28; joel10274/iStockphoto, 20; Public Domain, 21, 26; Andrés Álvarez Iglesias CC2.0, 23; breakermaximus/iStockphoto, 24; Andreas Gradin/Shutterstock Images, 27

Library of Congress Cataloging-in-Publication Data
Names: Morey, Allan, author.
Title: 12 terrifying monsters / by Allan Morey.
Other titles: Twelve terrifying monsters
Description: Mankato, MN : 12-Story Library, 2017. | Series: Scary and spooky
   | Includes bibliographical references and index.
Identifiers: LCCN 2016002357 (print) | LCCN 2016006723 (ebook) | ISBN
   9781632352972 (library bound : alk. paper) | ISBN 9781632353474 (pbk. :
   alk. paper) | ISBN 9781621434634 (hosted ebook)
Subjects: LCSH: Monsters--Juvenile literature.
Classification: LCC GR825 .M76 2016 (print) | LCC GR825 (ebook) | DDC
   001.944--dc23
LC record available at http://lccn.loc.gov/2016002357

Printed in the United States of America
Mankato, MN
May, 2016

Access free, up-to-date content on this topic plus a full digital version of this book. Scan the QR code on page 31 or use your school's login at 12StoryLibrary.com.

Table of Contents

Bakhtak Won't Let You Escape Your Nightmares

Nightmares are frightening. But to wake from a bad dream and not be able to move is terrifying! This feeling of being awake while unable to move is called sleep paralysis. It usually happens as people move between states of wakefulness and sleep. The body is still asleep while the mind is awake for a moment. Anyone who has experienced this knows it can be scary.

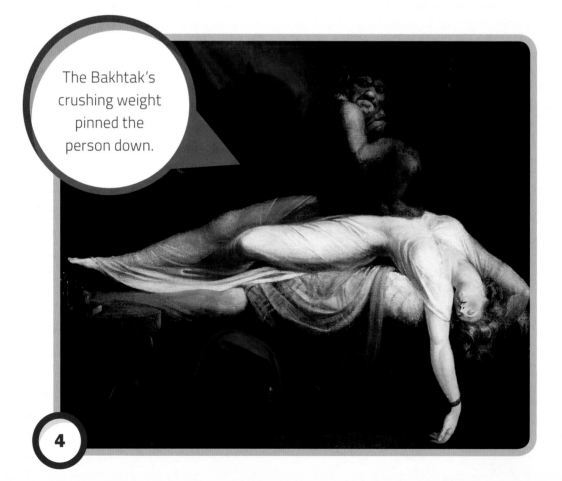

The Bakhtak's crushing weight pinned the person down.

The Bakhtak would sit and watch the person's suffering.

Ancient peoples did not know what caused sleep paralysis. They thought evil spirits were to blame. In Persian myths, that spirit was the Bakhtak. Stories said these goblin-like creatures enjoyed watching people suffer from their nightmares.

People believed that once a person fell asleep, a Bakhtak would climb onto his or her chest. They could not move even if they woke. The person felt a great pressure on his or her chest. He or she had trouble breathing. Or they felt an evil presence nearby. Then, as the person fell back to sleep, his or her fear caused a nightmare.

Other cultures have stories of monsters similar to the Bakhtak. In Great Britain, a witch called the Old Hag caused nightmares. In Scandinavian myths, creatures called mares caused bad dreams. In Thailand, Phi Am was to blame. This evil spirit sat on people's chests while they slept.

4

Estimated number of evil spirits once believed to cause sleep paralysis and nightmares.

- In Persian myths, this evil spirit was the Bakhtak.
- In Thailand, a ghostly spirit called Phi Am sat on people while they slept.
- In Great Britain, the Old Hag caused people's nightmares.
- In Scandinavia, mares gave people bad dreams.

Venomous Basilisk Is World's Deadliest Creature

The basilisk is a terrifying creature from myth. It was called the king of snakes. It earned this nickname because of the crown-like crest on its head. The basilisk was said to be the most venomous animal ever to have lived. It could kill with its gaze. Even its breath was deadly.

This form of the basilisk is often called a cockatrice.

The basilisk has been described in many ways. It is a huge lizard in some

stories. In others, it is a slithering snake. The most interesting description is a mash-up of animals. The basilisk was said to have the head, wings, and feet of a rooster. It had the body and tail of a dragon.

Basilisks are said to have lived in deserts. Their poisonous breath and deadly gaze killed everything around them. This included plants and animals. Basilisks turned the land where they lived into a wasteland.

Luckily, these deadly creatures of myth had some weaknesses. They died if they saw their own reflections. Weasels were also said to be safe from their gaze.

Basilisks and their deadly powers have fascinated people for ages. Mentions of them appear in plays by William Shakespeare. Leonardo da Vinci lists them in his book *Bestiary*. More recently, one of the Harry Potter books has a snake-like basilisk.

77 CE
Year of one of the earliest mentions of basilisks in writing.

- Basilisks are known as kings of the snakes.
- They could kill with their gaze and their breath.
- Basilisks have been given many different descriptions throughout the years.
- They could die by looking at their reflections.

GREEN BASILISK LIZARD

Often, names from myths get used for modern-day things. For example, most of the planets are named after Roman gods. Today, the green basilisk lizard lives in Central America. It does not strike fear in anyone. But it is an amazing animal. It can run across water with its webbed feet. Why is it called a basilisk? It has a crest on its head, similar to the mythological basilisk.

Bigfoot Stomps Around the Woods

People have told stories of wild men for years. These tales are of untamed men. They are men who do not live by cultural rules. They are big, hairy, and smell bad. These men have been called many names, including Sasquatch, Yeti, and Yowie. The common name is Bigfoot.

Bigfoot has been described as standing between 8 and 10 feet (2.4 and 3 m) tall and weighing up to 800 pounds (363 kg). He is covered in fur. Some people say Bigfoot looks similar to a cross between a man and an ape.

The recent interest in Bigfoot began in 1958. Loggers around Bluff Creek, California, noticed odd footprints in the woods. They were giant. The footprints were far apart.

Bigfoot earned his nickname from the large footprints he leaves behind.

16

Length, in inches (41 cm), of a rumored Bigfoot footprint.

- Bigfoot is said to be an untamed man.
- Bigfoot has different names, including Sasquatch, Yeti, and Yowie.
- It is said to be up to 10 feet (3 m) tall.
- Most Bigfoot sightings are in the Pacific Northwest.

There are reports of Bigfoot all over the United States and Canada.

The loggers imagined that they had to be made by a tall person, or creature, with a long stride. Jerry Crew, one of the workers, took a plaster cast of the prints. The local newspaper found out. This helped spread the story of Bigfoot around the world.

The Bluff Creek Bigfoot was discovered to be a trick. But that did not stop people from believing wild men were stomping around the woods. Most rumored sightings of Bigfoot are from the Pacific Northwest.

EPIC OF GILGAMESH

The *Epic of Gilgamesh* is believed to be the earliest work of western literature. It was written approximately 4,000 years ago. Gilgamesh was the unkind king of Uruk. As punishment for being mean, the gods sent Enkidu to fight Gilgamesh. Enkidu was the original wild man. Gilgamesh and Enkidu battled fiercely. The two became friends instead of enemies and went on several quests together.

4

Chupacabras Suck the Blood from Animals

Unlike most other terrifying monsters there are recent stories about chupacabras. But chupacabra legends started in the same way as stories of ancient beasts. Something happened that people did not understand. So they made up stories to explain events.

The first reported sighting of a chupacabra was in Puerto Rico. Livestock were reported killed. People said the animals' blood had been drained. As more livestock were found dead, stories spread about the beast that killed them. It was given the name chupacabra. This roughly translates to "goatsucker." Since then, chupacabra sightings have been reported across the United States. People have claimed to see them in Kentucky, Mississippi, and Texas. There are also reports of them being spotted in Central and South America.

The first reports of chupacabras described them with sharp quills running down their backs.

People first described chupacabras as lizard-like creatures. This image has changed as there have been more rumored sightings. Now chupacabras are described as being dog-like.

There are reports of people catching this terrifying creature, or something they believe is a chupacabra. So far, all of these critters have turned out to be odd-looking coyotes, foxes, or raccoons. The animals were believed to be suffering from mange. This skin disease causes hair loss.

Chupacabras have huge teeth that look similar to fangs.

THINK ABOUT IT

Urban legends are modern tales of strange things such as chupacabras. What is an urban legend that you have heard? What is a logical, more rational explanation behind this legend?

1995
Year of the first reported sighting of a chupacabra.

- Chupacabras are mythical creatures.
- The first sighting in Puerto Rico was after several livestock were killed.
- Sightings have been reported in the southern United States and Central and South America.
- All captured chupacabras have been confirmed to be other animals suffering from mange.

11

No One Escapes the Grim Reaper

There is one terrifying monster no one can escape. It is death. Everyone dies. So according to stories, death eventually gets us all.

Anubis was seen as a helpful god.

Death is also known as the Grim Reaper.

Death was not so grim in ancient times. In Greek myths, Thanatos was the god of death. In Egyptian myths, it was Anubis. These gods guided people's souls to the Underworld after they died. The Underworld is a mythical place where spirits of the dead go to rest.

The way people thought of death changed in the 1400s. The Black Plague spread across Europe. It was a horrific disease that killed millions. Instead of seeing death as a peaceful event, people now saw it as something terrible. Their view of death, the mythical figure, also changed.

The Grim Reaper was seen as a skeletal figure wearing black robes. In some stories, he holds an hourglass. The hourglass tells when someone is about to die. In his other hand the Grim Reaper

THINK ABOUT IT

What is the main idea of these two pages? List at least three pieces of evidence that support your choice.

carries a scythe. This bladed tool was normally used for harvesting crops. The Grim Reaper used it for collecting souls.

Stories vary about the Grim Reaper's job. Some say he kills people. But more commonly, it is believed that he "reaps" or collects people's souls after they die. Then he guides them to the afterlife.

1400s

Era when the idea of death became scarier than the ancient gods of death.

- Ancient people were not scared of death.
- The gods of death were seen as helpful because they took people's souls to the Underworld.
- After the Black Plague, people's views of death changed.
- The Grim Reaper is a skeletal figure that people believed would appear when they were about to die.

If people see the Grim Reaper, it means they are about to die.

Kraken Lurks in the Ocean's Depths

The Kraken is another monster with roots in ancient myths. Stories describe it as a tentacled sea monster. It looks similar to a giant squid or octopus.

In Greek myths, Poseidon was the god of the sea. He had a terrible sea monster. Some stories call his monster a ketos. If anyone angered Poseidon, he called this beast to seek revenge. Few people survived the ketos's wrath.

Stories of this sea monster were more common in Scandinavian myths. Giant squid live in the northern Atlantic Ocean. They can grow to be huge. There is a strong possibility that giant squid encouraged rumors of the Kraken. If a person long ago saw a giant squid,

The Kraken was said to destroy many ships in the ocean.

he or she might have thought it was the Kraken.

The Kraken has made many appearances in books and movies. Jules Verne included one in *20,000 Leagues Under the Sea*. A Kraken also makes an appearance in the movie *Pirates of the Caribbean: Dead Man's Chest*.

The giant squid could easily have been confused for the Kraken.

43

Length, in feet (13 m), to which a giant squid can grow.

- The Kraken is a tentacled sea monster from myths.
- The god Poseidon is said to have had control over the ketos.
- It was common in Scandinavian myths.
- The Kraken has been featured in books and movies.

KILLING THE KETOS

Poseidon was an angry god. Once, Queen Cassiopeia said her daughter, Andromeda, was more beautiful than Poseidon's sea nymphs. In anger, the god told Cassiopeia she had to sacrifice Andromeda to the ketos. If she did not, her kingdom would be destroyed. Luckily for Andromeda, the hero Perseus came along and saved the day by killing the ketos.

Monster Seen in Loch Ness, Scotland

Loch Ness is a long, narrow lake in Scotland. It is also said to be the home of Nessie, a dinosaur-like monster. Rumors of large creatures in Scotland's lakes have scared people for hundreds of years. Early on, these beasts were called water horses or kelpies. They were rumored to offer rides to children. Anyone who went with them would never be seen again. The Loch Ness Monster was among these legendary creatures.

Nessie was first seen around 1,500 years ago. But the real excitement over her existence began in the early 1900s. In 1933, two people claimed to have seen a large animal splashing around in the water. Their story was printed in a local newspaper. Soon, the obsession over Nessie spread.

Loch Ness is one of the largest and deepest lakes in the United Kingdom.

Some videos and photos have been taken throughout the years. They are all blurry.

Many people have reported seeing the Loch Ness Monster. In 1934, Colonel Robert Wilson claimed to have taken a picture of Nessie. It is one of the most famous photos of Nessie. It shows a dinosaur-like creature poking its head out of the water. Years later, a man named Tim Dinsdale wanted to prove Nessie was real. He said he took a video of the monster. The photos and videos of Nessie are fuzzy. It is unclear whether they really show the Loch Ness Monster.

The hunt for the Loch Ness Monster has continued over the years. Some have taken photos and video of what they claim is Nessie. Others have spent years searching for proof that she exists. But so far, no one has provided scientific evidence of her existence.

1960
Year of the most recent Loch Ness Monster video footage.

- Loch Ness is a lake in Scotland that is the supposed home of Nessie.
- Early water horses were said to offer rides to children who were never seen again.
- Two people claimed to have seen Nessie in 1933.
- People have spent years trying to spot the Loch Ness Monster.

Angry Goddess Curses Medusa

In myths, Medusa was a horrific monster. But she did not start out that way. She once was a beautiful woman. Even the Greek gods on Mount Olympus admired her. Then she angered Athena, the goddess of war. Medusa was in love with Poseidon, the god of the sea. He was Athena's biggest rival.

Athena could not harm the powerful Poseidon. He was a god. She cursed Medusa instead. Medusa's fair skin turned scaly. Her fingers became sharp, brass talons. Her hair turned into venomous snakes. Anyone who met her gaze was petrified with fear. They would turn to stone.

As a horrifying monster, Medusa set up her lair in Africa. Myths said she lived in a cave with her even scarier sisters, Stheno and Euryale.

MYTH TYPES

There are many myth types. Creation myths explained how ancient peoples thought the world was created. Nature myths described natural events, such as what causes the winds to blow or the seasons to change. Quest myths were tales about heroes. Often, these heroes had to go on long, dangerous journeys. They faced terrifying monsters similar to Medusa.

Medusa was mortal. She could be killed. But her sisters were immortal. They could not be killed. They could even fly.

Outside Medusa's lair was a rock garden. It was filled with stony statues of people looking terrified. They were often caught mid-scream. They were Medusa's victims. These were the people who had met her gaze and turned to stone.

Medusa met her death when the hero Perseus was challenged to cut off her head. Instead of looking directly at her, he used his bronze shield as a mirror. This protected him from her stony gaze.

It is said the hero Perseus killed Medusa by cutting her head off.

2
Number of sisters Medusa had.

- Medusa was in love with Poseidon, Athena's biggest rival.
- Athena cursed Medusa, making her hideous with hair made of snakes.
- Her gaze could turn people to stone.
- Perseus killed Medusa, avoiding her gaze by using his shield as a mirror.

Vampires Want to Suck Your Blood

Ghosts, ghouls, and mummies are frightening undead creatures. But none of them are as terrifying as vampires. Legends of these bloodthirsty creatures have haunted people's nightmares for ages. There have been rumors of vampire-like monsters throughout Asia, Europe, and the Americas. But it was Bram Stoker's book *Dracula* that popularized these creatures of the night.

Vampires were first thought to be supernatural creatures or evil spirits. They fed off the living. But over time, legends change. A few hundred years ago, people believed in vampire-like creatures called revenants. They were said to be dead people who rose from their graves. These monsters fed on people. Then Stoker wrote his book.

The character of Dracula is based on Vlad Tepes, a Romanian prince. Tepes fought a bloody war to save his homeland. He was nicknamed Vlad the Impaler. Stories said he tortured and killed people by sticking them on sharpened poles. Now, Dracula is the basis for most modern beliefs about vampires. In his book, Stoker wrote that a

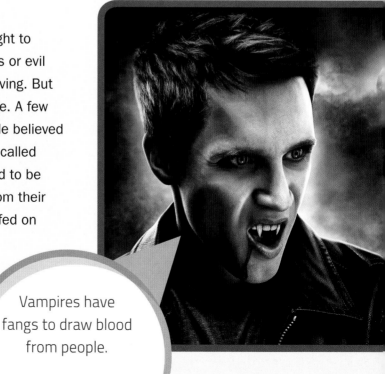

Vampires have fangs to draw blood from people.

person could be changed into a vampire by being bitten by a vampire.

Now, vampires are thought of as bloodthirsty monsters that prowl the night. They usually bite people's necks. Vampires are believed to be able to change form. They are said to change into bats, rats, or wolves.

Vampires do have some weaknesses. They cannot see their reflection in mirrors. The sunlight burns them. They also

Stoker used tales of Vlad's cruelty to develop the character Dracula.

have a strong reaction to garlic. People believe there are two ways to kill a vampire. One is to drive a stake through its heart. Another is to cut off its head.

1897
Year Bram Stoker's *Dracula* was released.

- Stoker's book made vampires popular.
- Dracula is based on Vlad Tepes, a Romanian prince.
- People believe that vampires prowl at night and feed on humans' blood.
- Vampires have weaknesses that include garlic and sunlight.

THINK ABOUT IT

As new stories are told about vampires, people's ideas about them change. Does your view of vampires differ from the text? How so? What stories helped you develop your opinions about vampires?

The Curse of the Wendigo

Sometimes monsters are created through a curse. In myths, this usually happens when a person commits a horrible act. Sometimes a mythical god punishes the person. Other times a spirit does it. That is the case with the wendigo.

Legends of wendigos are of American Indian origin. The Inuit in Alaska and the Algonquin in eastern Canada have told stories of this terrifying beast. These tribes lived in cold, wintry climates. They stayed in remote areas.

During the harshest winters, it was difficult to find food. To survive, there were rumors of people resorting to cannibalism. They would eat the flesh of another human being. People were cursed for this horrific act. They would be turned into wendigos.

Wendigos were huge, evil beasts. They had hearts of ice. They are thought to have ice surrounding them. Once they had the taste for human flesh, they could not stop eating people. They were thought to be selfish and greedy.

1878

Year of one of the first known Western cannibalism incidents.

- Wendigos are created from a curse.
- They are an American Indian legend.
- Wendigos appear after people resort to cannibalism.
- Once they start tasting human flesh, they cannot stop.

Wendigos exist only in cold, arctic places.

11

Werewolves Hunt During the Full Moon

In ancient times, the full moon was rumored to be a time when crazy things happened. Spirits were strongest then. It is when they roamed the earth. Some of these creatures were called lycanthropes, or shape-shifters. The most feared of them were werewolves.

In Europe during the 1500s, men were often accused of being werewolves. Werewolves could turn their skin inside out. But as tales of

Werewolves appear during full moons.

OTHER LYCANTHROPES

In Europe, people feared and hated wolves. Wolves ate their livestock. People even believed that hungry wolves would attack them. Their fears helped fuel rumors of deadly werewolves. But in Asia and Africa, people feared tigers and lions. So instead of werewolves, they told tales of werecats. There are also stories of wererats and werepigs.

werewolves became part of popular culture, the stories changed.

In 1846, *Wagner, the Wehr-Wolf* by George W. M. Reynolds told of a man who had been cursed to turn into a wolf every full moon. In the 1935 movie *Werewolf of London*, a man changes into a werewolf after being bitten. A year later, French author Abel Chevalley retold the story of the *Beast of Gévaudan.* In his retelling, a werewolf is killed by a silver bullet. These ideas helped create the terrifying creatures people know today.

30,000
Estimated number of people who claimed or appeared to be werewolves between 1520 and 1630 in France.

- It was believed that evil spirits, including werewolves, roamed Earth during full moons.
- In the 1500s, people believed that some men were werewolves.
- As werewolves became more popular, their descriptions changed.
- People who become werewolves at night do not remember what they did.

If someone is a werewolf, it is believed he or she will go through a change when there is a full moon. The person loses control of his or her body. His or her face extends into a snout. Hair sprouts all over the body. The next day, they will not remember what they did during the night as werewolves.

Zombies Gather in Deadly Hordes

Similar to vampires, zombies are undead creatures. Stories of zombies have also changed greatly over time. It was first believed that zombies were created by voodoo magic. A spell would reawaken a dead body. It would rise from its grave. The undead creature was mindless and slow. And it would be under the control of whoever cast the spell.

The movie *Night of the Living Dead* helped create modern ideas of zombies. They are still seen as lumbering, undead creatures. But in the movie, zombies had an uncontrollable hunger for human flesh. This hunger drove them to attack and kill people. Anyone bitten by a zombie then became one.

Instead of magic, a disease now turned living people into zombies. This idea made these undead creatures even more terrifying. But it

THEY WON'T STAY DEAD!

NIGHT OF THE LIVING DEAD

They keep coming back in a bloodthirsty lust for HUMAN FLESH!...

Pits the dead against the living in a struggle for survival!

The *Night of the Living Dead* popularized modern zombies.

also made them more popular to the public. There has been a continuous stream of new zombie movies and television shows in recent years.

Usually, a single zombie is not a threat. It is slow and easy to avoid. But the idea that a disease can transform masses of people into zombies is scary.

1968
Year *Night of the Living Dead* was released.

- Zombies are undead creatures.
- They were created by voodoo magic.
- Popular culture changed zombies to be flesh-eating creatures.
- A horde of zombies is impossible to escape.

A horde of zombies is impossible to escape.

Fact Sheet

- Myths and legends are different. Myths were once used to explain why things happened. Ancient peoples may have believed them. But now we know that myths are not true. Legends are stories based on truth, or at least what people think is true. There is no scientific proof to back up these stories. For example, Medusa is a creature of myth. There is no evidence she ever existed. There are only stories of her. Bigfoot is a legend. People have claimed to see him. People have taken photos that they say show Bigfoot. But that is not strong enough proof to say Bigfoot truly exists.

- Long ago, people used myths to explain what they did not understand. Some stories described how natural disasters happened. They were tales of storms and earthquakes. Others explained things that scared people. For example, people did not know why they had scary dreams. They blamed evil spirits for their nightmares. People told stories about how these creatures gave them bad dreams.

The Greek hero Perseus cut off Medusa's head. But the tale of Perseus and Medusa did not end there. He had to carry her head home to complete his quest. Myths say blood from Medusa's head fell in the Sahara Desert as Perseus flew over Africa. When the drops of blood hit the sand, they sizzled and hissed. Then venomous snakes sprouted. This story explains why there are so many snakes in deserts.

People do not believe in most monsters. But Bigfoot, Nessie, and chupacabras are different. There have been recent reported sightings of these creatures. People are more likely to think they are real. In fact, there are Bigfoot and Loch Ness Monster organizations. These groups post news about the monsters. They list recent sightings. There have also been television shows about Bigfoot and Nessie.

Glossary

ancient
Coming from or belonging to a time in the past.

culture
The beliefs and traditions of a group of people.

legend
An old story that is believed to be true but cannot be proven.

logger
Someone who cuts down trees for wood.

myth
A story told by ancient peoples to explain the world, as they understood it.

paralysis
Loss of the body's ability to move caused by illness, poison, or injury.

sea nymphs
Female spirits that live in the sea.

venomous
Capable of putting poison into another animal's body by biting or stinging.

voodoo
A religion mostly practiced in Haiti.

For More Information

Books

Chambers, Catherine. *Bigfoot*. Chicago: Heinemann, 2016.

Hoena, Blake. *Everything Mythology*. Washington, DC: National Geographic, 2014.

Morey, Allan. *Werewolves*. Minneapolis: Abdo, 2014.

Niver, Heather Moore. *Dracula: and Other Vampires*. New York: Rosen, 2016.

Visit 12StoryLibrary.com

Scan the code or use your school's login at **12StoryLibrary.com** for recent updates about this topic and a full digital version of this book. Enjoy free access to:

- Digital ebook
- Breaking news updates
- Live content feeds
- Videos, interactive maps, and graphics
- Additional web resources

Note to educators: Visit 12StoryLibrary.com/register to sign up for free premium website access. Enjoy live content plus a full digital version of every 12-Story Library book you own for every student at your school.

Index

About the Author

Allan Morey grew up in central Wisconsin. His early love of animals and making up stories led him to a career in writing. Some of his favorite things to write about are animals, sports, ghosts, and monsters. Currently, he lives in Minnesota with his wife, two kids, and pets.